SQL

The Ultimate Guide to Programming in SQL for Beginners, with Exercises for Learning SQL Languages and the Coding, Easily and in a Short Time (Step-by-Step Guide)

Daniel Géron

Table of Contents

By reading this document, the reader agrees that under no circumstances is the author responsible for any losses, direct or indirect, which are incurred as a result of the use of information contained within this document, including, but not limited to, — errors, omissions, or inaccuracies.

Introduction

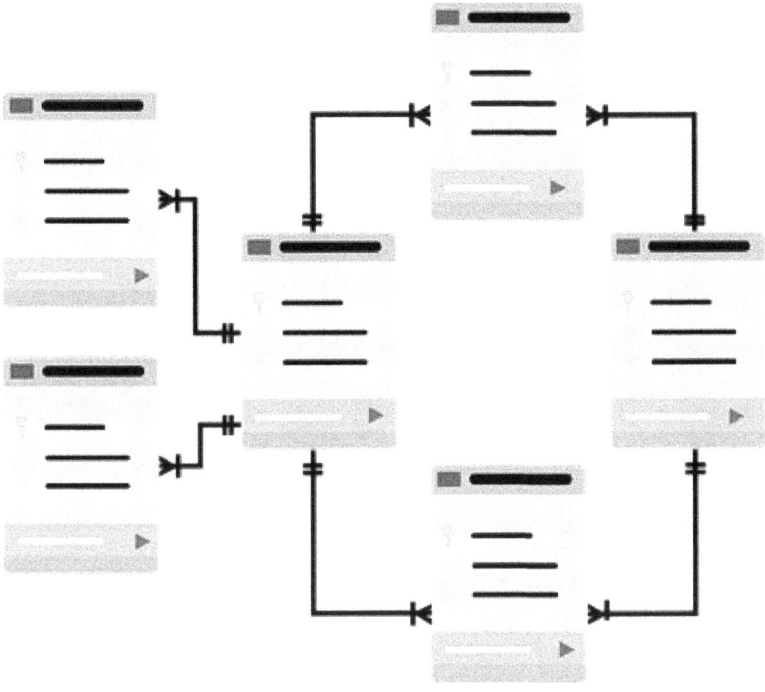

Congratulations on purchasing *SQL* and thank you for doing so.

The following chapters will discuss all of the different parts that you need to know in order to use the SQL language. If you are a large business or even one that is more medium in size, there are going to be times when you will work with a database. Whether you are handling customer information, transactional information, or something else, this database is going to handle a ton of the data that you need in a short amount of time.

When you have this database created and holding onto all of that information that is so valuable to your company, it is also important at times to be able to sort through it and see what is inside. If that database is really large, this could end up being a big problem. If you have millions of points in your database, do you really want to go through and try to find what you want out of that database? This is where the SQL language is going to come into play. It will help us to take control of the database, and find everything that we want with just a few simple commands.

You may hear that this is a programming language and worry that it is going to be too hard for you to get started because your experience with this is limited. The good news is that SQL is pretty simple to learn how to work with, and it is not going to take too long before you are able to get all of this down. We will take a look at a few of the codes that you are able to work within this language, and how easy they are. And all of the codes that you want to work within SQL will be the same way.

This guidebook is going to take some time to look at SQL and what we are able to do with this language for our databases overall. You will find that this is going to be an easy coding language to work with, and it is going to make some of the work that we are doing with these databases as painless and effortless as possible. Many businesses work with databases and being able to make this database work for our needs, and being able to pull up the right things when we or the user needs them can be critical as well.

There are a lot of different parts that come with the SQL language, and we are going to spend some time learning about these and how we can make it work for our needs. We will explore what the SQL language is all about, some of the most common commands that you can do with this language, how to work with the operators and even some of the functions. These can all come together to help us gain a better understanding of the SQL language and how we are able to use it in this guidebook.

We can then move on to some of the benefits of a relational database, which is what we would be able to work with when we want to handle SQL language, and even how to work on keeping our database as safe and secure as possible. If you are a large business that is planning on selling items online, then you want to make sure the information about your customers, about what they purchased in the past, and their transactional data is kept safe and sound. This part of the guidebook is going to help us to learn how we can keep that information safe so that only the people who should be using that part of the database. And it can help to keep your trust with the customers, and your own reputation, high and intact as well.

We will then end this guidebook with a look at some of the real-life applications of this kind of language. We are going to take some time to see how we can take some of the coding and some of the other work that we have done in this guidebook, and look at how we are able to really use this language in the real world rather than just seeing a few of the options and thinking that there is no way to use this in our lives. All businesses that use a database will find that the SQL language is going to be one of the best options to help us see some success with working on that database.

Working with a database is one of the best things that a company is going to be able to use when it is time to organize their transactions, their products, and some of the customers they are working with as well. And the SQL language is going to be a big deal when it is time to work with this database and how you are able to make all of this work together. When you are ready to work with SQL and seeing what difference it can do with some of your own databases, make sure to check out this guidebook to see how it can work for your needs.

There are plenty of books on this subject on the market, thanks again for choosing this one! Every effort was made to ensure it is full of as much useful information as possible, please enjoy it!

Chapter 1: What is SQL?

Welcome to the world of SQL! We are going to spend some time in this guidebook learning more about the SQL language, what we are able to do with it, and why it is such a great language for us to learn how to use overall. When you want to work with databases and organizing the information that is inside of them, then this is one of the best places for you to get started with overall.

There are many businesses out there that you are able to spend your working years with. Some are going to be smaller and may only come with a few employees. And then there are those who are really large and will have more than one office and be spread out around the world. But no matter what kind of company we are working with when you look at some of the structure that comes with it, you will notice that this business is going to generate, and then hold and use, data of some sort.

All of these companies are going to choose their method of holding onto this information and using it as well. And sometimes it is going to be determined based on the regulations that are going on around them. But one of the more traditional methods that we are able to use with this one is going to be known as the Database Management System. This is a great option to ensure that all of that data we want to hold onto is going to stay in one place and be easier to look through and use when needed.

The DBMS systems are going to be simple ones that we are able to choose from, and we will find that they have been around for many years already. But there are a few other methods, ones that are sometimes considered better, that have changed the way that many companies are able to hold onto their information. Even some of the most basic of these systems have seen some changes in order to add in some more power than they were able to use in the past.

It may seem like this is not something that we need to worry about all that much. Why would we need a database that is powerful or has some more features? But in reality, this is going to be helpful to those companies that want to store a lot of data, and they need to make sure that they are able to keep track of that information, or even with those companies that have to really handle the data carefully because it contains information that is more sensitive.

Because of all of the changes that have come up in the ways that these types of data should be stored overall, there is now going to be a new type or a new breed of data management that most companies are able to use. This is going to be known as the Relational Database Management System and it is one that is derived on that DBMS that we talked about before, but with some changes that come with it. It is going to come with a lot of new features with client technologies and things that you are able to do online with it. It is a great way to make sure that companies are really able to manage some of the data that they are working with.

While there are still quite a few systems that we are able to use for handling this data and for making sure that we get these databases down, you will notice that most companies can agree that SQL is one of the best options out there. this is because it is one of the easiest ones that we can use, and it is going to help us to keep all of the information that we have safe and secure. That is why we are going to devote some of our time to this guidebook learning more about SQL and how this language is able to benefit us.

What is SQL?

The first thing that you need to ask is what is SQL. SQL is going to stand for Structured Query Language and it is a pretty basic language that you can use in order to interact with the different databases that are on your system. The original version did come out in the 70s, but it has really started to see some changes when IBM released a new prototype that released SQL to the world.

This first particular tool was called ORACLE and it was so successful that the part of the company that worked with ORACLE was able to break off from IBM and started off on their own. ORACLE is still one of the leaders in the programming language field because it works with SQL and continuously makes it easier for people to learn how to work with the database.

When you are working with SQL, you are going to see that the databases are basically groups of information. Some will consider these databases to organize mechanisms that are able to store the information that the user will be able to access at a later time, effectively and efficiently, helping the business to get the information that they need without having to worry about issues coming up.

There are a lot of times that you are already using databases like the ones you find in SQL without even realizing that you are using them. For example, if you have ever used a phone book, you are using a type of database because it is going to contain a lot of information about people that can help you to sort them out, such as the names, phone numbers, and even their addresses. It is even in alphabetical order so it is easier for everyone to find out the information, also known as the pieces of data, that you need in no time. The SQL database is going to work in a similar manner to help you keep track of the information that your business needs.

The relational database

The first type of database that we are going to take a look at here is going to be known as the relational databases. These are the ones that are going to help us out because we can segregate them into tables or other logical units. These tables can be interconnected inside the database that we are using at that time. this database is also helpful because it is going to make it easier for us to break up any of the data that we want, breaking it into smaller units that you are able to manage easier, while also optimizing them to make it a bit easier to work on overall.

Now, it is important for a programmer to know more about the relational database because this is going to be the key that can help you to keep all of your information together, but it also helps s to split up that data into smaller pieces that are easier for us to read through if we need. The server, when we use the right commands, is able to go through all of these parts to see what you need because it also sees these smaller pieces are easier to go through compared to some of the bigger ones. Because of all of the optimization that you are able to add in, and the efficiency that is found in this system, it is common that a business, when they need to work with some large amounts of data and a database, will work with SQL rather than choosing one of the other options that are out there.

The client and server technology

For a long time, a lot of the computers that various businesses were using in the industry would be known as mainframe computers. This means that the machines were going to hold up a large system that was great for helping us to process and store the information that we needed. The user was able to use these computers and then interact with the mainframe using what was done on the dumber terminal, or on one that doesn't think on their own without the programmer doing some of the thinking. In order to make sure that we are able to get that terminal to get the right kinds of functions to perform, it is going to rely on memory, storage, and processing that all happen inside of that computer system instead.

While these systems did work and have been used for a long time, and there isn't necessarily something wrong with the setup (we can still find that many companies today are going to use these to help them get a lot of things done in their business), there really are a lot of better solutions out there. Solutions that are going to help us to get the job done a lot faster, and in a more efficient manner than we are able to find with some of the mainframe options that were used in the past.

And one of these options is going to be the client and server systems. These systems are going to work with a different kind of process in order to help us to get the results we want out of the database. In this one, the main computer, which is the server part, can be accessed by the user that is already on the network.

For the most part, they are going to access this network through either the LAN or the WAN network that they have.

The user also has the option of getting onto and accessing the server from their desktop computer or from another server, rather than having to rely on these dumb terminals that were so popular in the past. Every computer, which is going to be the client in this kind of system, is able to access this system. This allows for easier and smoother interactions between the clients and the server to get things done.

Database Systems Online

While the client and server technology are something that a lot of businesses are going to rely on, and it is one that has worked for a very long time, there are more people who are moving to add in more integration between the Internet and their databases than ever before. This kind of system is going to allow the user a way to access their database when they go online so that they will be able to be on their own web browser at the time, checking out the database when it works for them.

Customers, as well as others who would like to either use or check out the data that is there, is able to get online, with the right credentials and information, and make some changes to the account, check on transactions, look at the inventories, purchase items, pay online, and more. All of this is something that we are able to do from the web browser, and the customer can even do this from their own home, or anywhere else that they would like, which is going to allow the system to run smoothly.

To work with this kind of database for some of your needs, you will simply need to start out with a web browser, anyone that works the best for you, and then go to the website of the company you want to use to access that database. Often these companies are going to have you use login details so that you can go to the part of the database that relates to you the most. Then you can work with the search function to find any of the information that you want. We think of this as looking through our account, but it is a big database that we are able to use.

Many of these online databases are going to help keep our information safe at the same time and will ensure, through some login credentials, that we are only able to access our information and none of the information of other users on that database. If you have to purchase an item or you have to make a payment, then these log in requirements are going to be there. Most of the time you can log in for free, but this ensures that your information is going to stay safe and sound and that no one else is going to be able to access what is there.

Of course, while this system sounds pretty easy to handle, there are going to be many things that happen on the system that works behind the scenes to get them up and running. The customer will be able to access a bit of the basic information, such as their payment information and past order history, there is going to be a lot that the server is going to need to put together to make this information show up in an easy to read format on the screen.

For example, you may see that the web browser that you are using is going to use and execute SQL in order to figure out what data the user wants to see. SQL will also be used in order to reach the database that the customer has put in place on the system, such as food or clothing that they want to see, and then SQL will be able to send this information back to the website before showing it all on the web browser for the user.

This is something that can take a bit of time to put together and get to work, but it is going to be a great system that runs well that can help make sure that the user gets onto the system in just a few seconds if it is working in the proper manner. All of the things that we have already discussed above SQL can happen in just a few seconds, and can show up with something as simple as a search result, or when the customer is looking over their own payment information. It may seem like a simple action to you to get there, but a ton of information is coming up in the background, and a lot of different parts have to come together to make this all happen. And that is the beauty of working with the SQL system.

The Advantages of Using SQL

Now that we have a bit of information on the SQL language and some of the background of how this works, it is time to take a look at some of the advantages that come with this system. When it comes to picking out a language that you want to use for coding, there are going to be a few options. All of these do work in different manners based on what you would like to do with them and sometimes the reason that you may go with one is because of your preferences or because one is better at a task than the other.

We are going to spend our time in this guidebook learning about the SQL language and what we are able to do with it when it comes to our databases. There are a lot of benefits that we are going to see when it comes to working with the SQL language in order to help us to get a database set up and ready to go. Some of the benefits that we are going to notice when we are working on this kind of language include:

- High speed—if you are looking for something that is high speed, the SQL option is one of the best. The SQL queries are able to retrieve a lot of information from the database in just a little bit of time and it is one of the most efficient options that you are able to use on the market to get this done.

- Well defined standards—the SQL databases have been around for some time and they have some good standards that will help to make it easier to keep the database nice and strong. Some of the other databases don't have these clear standards and it can make it difficult to store the information that you need.

- No coding needed—you are able to use the SQL system in order to store some of the information for your business without knowing a lot of coding ahead of time. You will learn a few parts of coding inside of this guidebook to do the right commands, but you don't need to have extensive knowledge of coding before getting started.

- The emergence of object-oriented DBMS—the earlier SQL databases were based on the relational databases and while this is not a bad thing, there are some better and faster options. Now they are moving on to some of the newer options to help get the work done, including with object-oriented DBMS to help out.

While there are going to be a ton of benefits that we are able to see when it comes to working with this kind of coding language to help us with our databases, there are also some disadvantages or thins that we are not going to like about the SQL language. And there are reasons why we may decide to go with another type of language to help our databases. Some of the reasons that a programmer may decide to not go with this kind of language will include:

- Difficult with the interface—even though you don't need to know how to work with coding before getting started with the SQL coding language, it is sometimes harder to interface with this kind of database. This database is a bit more complex to interface compared to just working with a few lines of code like you would be able to do with some of the other coding languages.

- Features that need 3rd parties—there are some features that are added in with SQL that will need to have a 3rd party to ensure vendor lock-in. if you don't want to bring in some other parties to this because of the information that you are storing, you will need to consider going with another option.

SQL is one of the best tools to use to make this all happen. It is the way that you will be able to use and store the information so that when a user does a search on the website or some other action, the right information is going to get sent back to them. We will spend some time in this guidebook talking about how SQL will be able to do this along with some of the other great features and tools that you will learn about when it comes to using SQL to store the information and data for your company.

Chapter 2: Some of the Commands That You Can Get Started With

Now it is time for us to dive into some of the fun things that we get to do with this kind of coding language. We are going to look at some of the commands that we are able to do when it comes to working with the SQL language and how we can actually search through our databases and see what information is inside as much as possible. In this chapter, we are going to take a look at how we can work with SQL and some of the basic commands that we can use to make these work for our needs.

These commands are helpful because they will make it easier to work with the different parts that we want in that database. We will find that some of these are going to be easy commands to work with and then from there we are able to move on to some of the commands that are more difficult and complicated so that we can see some of the power that it comes to working in this kind of language.

When it is time for you to learn some of the more basic commands that are available in SQL, you will find that the best way to deal with them is to divide them up into six separate categories. All of these categories are going to be based on what you are really able to use them for the inside of your chosen system. Below are going to be the six options of categories of commands that will work in the SQL language to help you to get things done with your codes.

Data Definition Commands

The first type of commands that we are going to look at is known as DDL, or data definition language. This is one of the aspects that is found inside of the SQL language that is going to make it easier for us to generate objects in the database before we go through and arrange them the way that we would like. For example, you would then be able to use this part of our SQL system to help s to delete or add objects to the table that we are making. Some of the different commands that will work with the DDL category here will include:

1. The drop view
2. The drop index
3. Alter the index
4. Create the index
5. Alter the table in some manner
6. Create the table
7. Drop the table.

Data Manipulation Language

The second part that we are going to take a look at here is going to be known as the DML, or the data manipulation language. This is going to be the aspect of SQL that we are able to use when we would like to be able to modify some of the information about the objects that are found in the database that you are using. This is going to make it easier to delete the objects, update these objects, or insert something new inside of the database. This is going to give us a lot of freedom when we want to make sure that the right changes to our information in the database are added in without having to make a new part of the table for this database.

Data Query Language

Now we need to move on to the Data Query Language, or the DQL as you are most likely to hear it called. This language is going to be one of the most powerful aspects that you are going to see with SQL, especially when you are working with a more modern database system for your business.

This one can be nice because you will only need to handle one easy command in order to choose what you want off of the database, and the command is the Select command. You can work with the Select command to help run some queries when they are needed inside of any relational database. If you would like to have it so that the results that come out are going to be more detailed, then it is possible to go through and add in some options or clauses to get this to all work out for you.

Data Control Language

Next on the list is going to be the DCL or the Data Control Language. This is going to be a command that you will be able to choose to work with any time that you want to have some control over the people who can be on that database or who can access it. The DCL command is used in some cases in order to generate the database objects related to who has access to see this information. This could include who will have the right to distribute privileges of access to the data. This is a good thing to use if your business is dealing with a lot of sensitive information and you only want a few people to be able to get ahold of it. Some of the commands that you may find useful to use when working with the DCL commands include:

- Revoke

- Grand

- Alter password

- Create synonym

Data Administration Commands

When you are working with the data administration commands, you are going to find that it allows you some power over the database that others are not able to have. you will be able to analyze, and when needed, audit, the operation that is going on in the database. In some cases, you will be able to use this to assess the overall performance of that database with the help of these specific commands.

This is going to be what can help to make these the right commands to work with when you would like to go through the system and fix some of the bugs that may be showing up in some of the work that you are doing. You will be able to work with these commands in order to get rid of these so that the database is able to work in the proper manner.

There are two options that come with these data administration commands and these include start audit and stop the audit. One thing that we do need to keep in mind when working with the database administration is that it is going to be different than the data administration when you are working with the SQL language. The database administration is going to make it easier for you to manage what is going on with the database, including some of the commands that can be used with SQL. It can also have some more specifics than the data administration when it comes to implementing the SQL language that you want.

The Transactional Control Commands

These are the good commands that you can use in SQL any time that you want to keep track of as well as manage the transactions that will happen inside the database. If you sell a product of any kind on your website, for example, you will need to use the transactional control commands to help keep track of these commands, keep track of the amount you are making, and to keep track of all the other things that you will need when working with those transactions. There are a few things that you will be able to do with these transactional control commands including:

- Commit—this one is going to save all the information that you have about the transactions inside the database.

- Savepoint—this is going to generate different points inside the groups of transactions. You should use this along with the Rollback command.

- Rollback—this is the command that you will use if you want to go through the database and undo one or more of the transactions.

- Set transaction—this is the command that will assign names to the transactions in your database. You can use it to help add in some organization to your database system.

As we can see as we go through this process, all of these commands are going to be important to what we want to get done within the code that we are writing out. these can help us to get some of the specific results that we are looking for inside of our database. And we will be able to take a bit more time to explore these and learn more about them as we go through this guidebook so that we can get a deeper look at what they are all about and how we are able to use them for some of our own needs as well. But this is a great way for us to get an introduction to what they are all about and how we can use them for some of our own needs as well.

Chapter 3: Are There Different Types of Data to Handle?

In any kind of coding language that you are going to spend your time on, you will find that working with the data types is going to be very critical to the amount of success that you are going to find with that language. We are going to spend some time here looking at how to work with some of the data types that come with SQL, and how we can use this to create new code in the process.

The data that we are working with and the types they are will really vary based on what you would like to do with the database at the time, as well as the different items that you may be trying to offer or sell to one of your customers. the data types that you are able to find inside of the SQL code are going o be the attributes that will match back up to the information that is found in that database. And then it is these characteristics that will be placed into a table so that it is easier to retrieve them and read through them easily.

A good example of how we are able to do this is when we require our database to have a field that is only able to hold onto numeric values, with n letters in it. You would be able to use some of the commands in SQL in order to set it up so that the user is limited to just adding in numbers to this field. This could happen when you want the credit card information or their zip code for example. This requirement can be a good thing to use because it will ensure that the user is putting in the right answer and doesn't make a mistake.

When we are able to assign the right data types to the fields that are found inside of your database, this is going to be a very good thing. You are ensuring with this one that there are going to be fewer errors in the data entry on the side of the customer that you are working within the process.

One thing that we need to remember here when we are working with SQL is that every version that you download and work with will come with a few different features and parts that you need to work with. This provides you with some different choices when it comes to the data types that you are working with. You will need to check out the rules of your version of SQL to make sure that this is all staying in order. For most parts, you will need to stick with using the data points that are going to work with your version of SQL to ensure that the database works in the right manner.

There are a few different options that we are able to work with here when it comes to the data types available, regardless of the version of SQL that you want to work with. Some of these are going to include character strings, time and date values, and numeric strings. Let's take a look at each one of these and see how they are going to work with some of the types of codes that you want to work with.

Working with Fixed Length Characters

The first data type that we are going to look at are the fixed length characters. If you have strings or constant characters that are going to be of constant length, you will need to make sure that you are saving them as a data type that is fixed length. The typical type of data that you will use for one of these when working in SQL will be:

CHARACTER(n)

The "n" is going to be the assigned length or the maximum length, that you want to allow on the field that you are working on. Perhaps you just want to allow the person to only put in 20 letters for their name or you want to keep the phone numbers from going on longer than they are allowed. This tool would help to make it a bit easier. You will need to input the information to determine how long you want the field to be before you get going. So, you can choose to just let the field be 20 characters long so with the syntax above, n would be 20. You can choose how long you would like it to be or just leave it open if the length doesn't matter.

You may also find that there are going to be a few of the SQL implementations that will work with the "CHAR" data type when you would like to save some of your information that is a fixed length. It is possible to work with this particular type of data at any time that you want to be able to save information that is considered alphanumeric at the time. so, if you would like to have them put their state name, but only the abbreviation of this, you would want to work with a fixed-length point of data so that they are only allowed to put in two letters in this field rather than spelling out the whole things.

When you decide to handle this kind of data, the user will be able to put in an answer, but that answer can never be longer than the number of data points that you used and what you set. With the example above, if the person lived in Florida, then they would be able to add in FL, but they would not be able to spell out the whole word of Florida.

When it is time to work with things like usernames and passwords, it is not a good idea to focus on these fixed data type lengths. You want to allow the user to have some freedom when they set up the username and password that they are going to work with for accessing your database. You can put on some other restrictions, such as saying they need to have a combination of letters and numbers here, or even that it needs to be a minimum of characters to be accepted, but do not put a maximum on this one. This will help them to pick out strong passwords that work for their needs.

Working with the Variable Characters

You will also have the option to use a varying length string in SQL. This is a string that can change in length depending on which data point that is being used. The standard notation that you can use for this particular option includes:

CHARACTER VARYING (n)

For this option, the "n" is going to be the number that identifies the assigned or the maximum, length of the field. There are a few types that you will be able to use when you want to work with variable characters including ANSI, VARCHAR2, and VARCHAR. VARCHAR is often the standard type of data that you would use when it comes to working with variable length characters but you are able to use some of the others if you would prefer.

These are going to be the types of data that will not come with some requirements for putting a certain number of spaces in it. For example, if the length of the field that we are working with is 15, then the user is only going to be able to put above that 15, but they could do fewer characters, such as 11, and the program would be just fine. The string is going to be able to go through and will change itself to just being 11 characters long when the user is all done.

Any time that you are doing something with a character string that is considered a variable, you need to make sure while doing this that you work with a data type that is of varying length. This is going to make it easier for us to maximize the space that you already have inside of the database, making it easier for the user to put in the right information, without errors or something else going on with the work either.

Numeric Values

The numeric value is always going to be stored inside the field as a number. These numerical values are sometimes going to be called by different names depending on their types, with names like real, decimal, integer, and number. Some of the standards with numerical values that you will be able to use inside the SQL system include:

- DECIMAL(p, s)

- REAL(s)

- BIT(n)

- FLOAT(p)

- INTEGER

- DOUBLE PRECISION(P)

- BIT VARYING(n)

We already discussed a bit before what "n" was gong to equal, but "p" is going to be the number that will show the assigned, or the maximum, number for the length of the field that you want. Also, you will notice that a few of the options above also use the "s". This is going to be used by the number that is already located on the right side of the decimal point.

The Decimal Points

First, we need to take a look at how we can work with some of the different types of numerical values that we have. we are going to start out with a look at the decimal point. These decimal points are just a numeric value that has a decimal point of some point found in it. You will just need to write out the decimal value in this kind of code as DECIMAL(p, s) so that it is going to show up as one of the SQL standards when you are doing the coding.

The precision that you are able to get with your decimal value is going to be the overall length of the numerical value. For example, if you have an answer that is going to show us as (5, 3), then this is going to show us that the precision is going to be 5. This is going to be the length that we are able to assign to our numeric value, and this one is going to be able to go up to 5 spaces behind the decimal point that is there.

Integers

Another option that we need to take a moment to look at is the integers. These are going to be some numeric values that will not have a decimal point in them at all. This means that they are going to be any of the numbers that we decide to work with that does not have a decimal point in it, and are considered whole numbers, whether this number is positive or negative is not going to matter. You will be able to use these in a lot of the codes that you are writing for SQL, and they can be used any time that you need to focus on a whole number without having a decimal point inside.

The floating-point decimal

The floating-point decimal is going to be a decimal value that has a precision and a scale that are in varying lengths. The floating-point decimal can have as many character lengths as you would like and it is not going to be limited by the characters. The data type that is called REAL is going to assign a column that will hold the single procession floating-point decimals. The data type that is called "DOUBLE PRECISION" will assign a column that will hold all the double-precision floating decimal points.

When it is time to determine whether or not this floating number is going to be seen as something with single or double precision in it, you will first need to take a look at the number that comes with it. If the precision is between one and 21, that means that you are dealing with a number that is considered single precision. But if you are working with a number that has a precision between 22 and 52, then you are dealing with a floating number that will rely on double precision.

Time and dates

The final part that we need to take a look at when it comes to these numerical values is the time and date and see how we are able to work with these in our database. These are going to be the types of data that will be able to record any data that is related to dates and time. The typical distributions that you see with SQL will be able to support a type of data that is known as DATETIME. But some of the other members that can come with this kind of option are going to include TIME, DATE, TIMESTAMP, INTERVAL.

Another option that we are able to see here is that you can work with some of the different elements when it comes to using any of the types that are above including the minute, hour, month, second, year and even day based on what your code needs to have happened.

The Literal Strings

The next part we are going to talk about is the literal strings. These are going to be the series of characters, like names or phone numbers, that are going to be specified by the program user or the database. For the most part, these strings are going to be full of data that has some similar characteristics. The value of the whole of the string will be identified together. The column's value is going to be unknown in many cases because there can be some different values that will exist between the data columns as well as between the data rows.

When you are working with literal strings, you will not be able to specify the types of data that you want to use. Rather, with these, you are going to specify the strings that you would like to use. Some of the examples of literal strings that you may notice when you are working with the SQL language include:

'August 1, 1990'
5.3
50000
Morning
"4500"

It is important for us to remember here that when we are working on a string that is considered alphanumeric, you will need to make sure that there are some quotation marks around the words. You get the choice on whether you are working with single or double quotation marks here though. The number of strings that you are using, whether large or small, will be stored without using these quotation marks, so it isn't that big of a deal really on how many you are using, but it is still a good thing to focus on a bit and see how it works.

The Null Values

The null values are going to show up in your code on occasion as well. These are going to basically be the missing values, or even missing columns, that are found inside one of the rows of data that you are working with. And they stand out because they will not have any kind of value inside of them. These values are important because they will play some kind of role in the SQL language that you are doing. You are able to take the null values in order to enter a literal string, to help create a table, and to assign new conditions for the search that you want to do.

If you decide that you would like to reference the null values, you can use the following method to help make this happen:

' ' (this will be the single quotation marks that have space in between them.)
NULL

When you are working with these null values, it is important to realize that you don't have to have data already entered into any of the fields. If you do have a scenario where the fields are asking for the data before you continue, you can use the data type that is then followed by the entry NOT NULL. If there is a possibility that this particular field won't need any data inside of it, you can make sure that you are using the null data type.

For example, if you are doing your work and find that you are able to leave a comment or an email inside of the system and you need to fill it out, you could use a null data type here. There are times when someone won't want to provide you with their email address, or they don't have one, and if you make them fill it out, then you will end up with them not being able to get on the system, or at least upset with you because they had to give up that information.

Allowing a few of these fields to stay empty on occasion, when they are not really all that necessary to the functioning of the system, can be helpful. But if there is a field that you need to use in order to learn about the customer, such as their name, then these needs to not be considered a null value along the way.

Boolean Values

Boolean values are an interesting part that we are able to use with a lot of different types of databases, and not just with them, but also with some of the other programming languages as well. When you decide to work with these Boolean values, you will find that there are really only three of them that you can use including null, true, or false.

You are able to work with the Boolean values at any time that you would like to look at and even compare some of the different units of the data. For example, if you would like to take some time to specify the parameters of a search, you would set it up so that all of the conditions that would show up in the results that we are doing will come back as null, false, or true based on what you put in as those conditions.

Keep in mind that with these values, it is only going to be able to retrieve the information when it deems it to be true. If the Boolean value ends up being false or null, it is not going to be retrieved for you or for the other person who is searching for it. However, if the value that comes up is seen as true, you will be able to get all of that information to show up. This is often the choice that is preferable when you are working with internet searches because it is going to help us to get the information that we need, rather than information that is not that important.

Stores that have products and services online will find that using these Boolean values will become one of the most efficient ways that the customer will be able to fill in some of the fields that are needed and do a search when they would like. It would not make all that much sense for you to simply list out all of the items on one page for the store unless you only have a few, and then hope that the customer will be able to find what they need. If your company sells more than just a few items, then this is going to backfire on you because it would take too long for the customer to find what they need.

With the help of these Boolean expressions though you will be able to set up the system so that it is going to retrieve the information that your customer is looking for the first time. Let's say that your customer is on your website and they are looking for a pink purse. They would be able to type this in and with the help of the Boolean expression, only the items that match both pink and purse will show up. If the items in the store are pink, but not a purse, then they won't show up. If the items are a purse, but not pink, they will not show up either.

There are other ways that we are able to apply these Boolean values, but this is one of the methods that we are able to use in order to really show how this can work out to help our customers. you are able to work with the Boolean values any time that you are hoping to search for some specific information inside of your store or the program you are working with, especially when we talk about the tables, and it is going to speed up the process you are using.

As we have spent some time talking about in this chapter, you can easily see that there are a ton of data types that we are able to work with and use when we want to make it easier to work in SQL. Each of these types of data will work in a manner that is slightly different and can make sure that you will get what you want out of the database, no matter how big it is.

Chapter 4: How to Manage Object in Your Database

Many of the coding languages that you will want to explore will have something to do with objects. You will find that working with these objects is going to ensure that we are able to really take care of our code and that the different parts are going to come together and work the way that we would like. That is why we are going to spend some time in this chapter learning a bit more about these objects and how we are able to make them work for our needs as well in SQL.

While we have already taken some of our time throughout the previous chapters to look over the different data types that we are able to explore in this language, and we have even gone through a few of the different commands that a programmer is able to rely on to get things done on your SQL databases and websites, it is now time to move on to the next step and look at how to handle some of the important objects that show up in SQL.

Some of the examples of the objects that show up in the different databases that we have and that you will learn more about through this chapter include sequences, synonyms, indexes, tables, clusters, and views. With this in mind, we are going to dive right in here and learn more about how we can work with some of these C++ objects to make things work better with our codes.

The Schema

Whenever you are working with something known as the schema, we have to remember that we are working with a set of objects that are found in our database that can be linked to just one, rather than to all, of the users of the database. The user of that particular schema will be known directly as the owner of the schema, and they will be the ones who will own the objects that are inside. The easiest way for them to get into that schema and use it for their own needs is to have a username and password associated back to it.

For example, anyone, even the user, will be able to generate an object, and then find that this same object is going to also generate in their own schema. This is a great way for that user to have more control over the objects in the database and can help us to see which ones can be generated, deleted, manipulated, and changed.

This is not going to be a small task when the user would like to get into their account and make a few changes to that area. An example of this is when one of your customers decides to sign up on your website and have their own account. They have signed up for this account with their own username and password, and the person who is considered the administrator of that database will approve both of these.

When the user has their own account, they can then go through and make the necessary changes to the system when they need. They may update their address when they move, and even what things they would like to order along the way as well. They will be able to get onto the account at any time that they want with the use of that username and password and can make any changes that are approved ahead of time by the administrator, to their own account, but not to any of the other accounts that are on that database as well.

Let's take a look at how this is going to work with an example. Let's say that you have all the credentials to login and your username for this example is going to be PERSON1. You are going to decide that you want to go into the database and work on creating a new table that you will call EMPLOYEES_TBL. When you go into your records, you are going to notice that the new table that you created is going to be called PERSON1.EMPLOYEES_TBL. The schema name is going to be the same as the person who created and owns the table.

When you feel like accessing a new schema that you are already the owner of, you will not need to use the name of the schema and you can just pull it up by using the name that you gave the table. But if you would like to pull up a table that someone else is the owner and creator of, you will need to use their username as the schema and place this in front of the table that you are looking to pull up.

Tools to Store Our Data

For the most part, you will find that when it is time to sore some of your information inside of any database you are working with, you will be able to work with a table format. The table is going to be pretty simple to work with and will consist of rows and columns that are given as much or as little space as you would like in the database. You get to be in control here by figuring out and choosing how much space they can take up, and whether that space is going to be considered permanent or temporary. Let's take a look at how these are meant to work a bit more in this chapter, to help us make sure that we are really getting them set up and that the tables are going to work the way that we want in our database.

Columns and Fields

To start with this, the files, which are going to be known as the columns when you are doing any work in our relational database, are going to be the parts of our table where you are able to assign the particular data type that you would like. You need to make sure that there is a name or something in the field that will match the data the best that you want to put into it. You need to also decide at this time whether the fields are allowed to be NULL or not, which means that the user is able to choose whether to put something in them or not, like with their email address. Or you can set them up to be NOT NULL which means that something has to be put into this part of the table or the code will not proceed.

When you are in the process of creating your own new table, all of these tables must have a minimum of one field. It is likely that you will end up with a lot of fields with most of the tables that you are working with, especially if you are trying to fill up the database with all of that new data that you have collected. The fields that come here are going to be in charge of storing the different types of data, including the addresses, phone numbers, and names of your customers.

Rows

While we are here, we also need to take a quick look at the rows. These are just going to be the records of data that you are able to find inside of the table that you were able to create above. For example, if you are working with a row that is for your customers in the database, this is going to be the part that will hold all of the information for the customer, including their phone number, name, address, order history and more. The rows will simply be composed of any fields that are able to hold all of the information for just one of the records that show up on your table.

Creating a New Table in SQL

When we reach this point, you may be a bit confused and will assume that when it is time to make our own new table, that it is going to be really hard, especially if you have some complex requirements. But SQL is a great language because it has made it easier than ever for you to create any kind of table that you would like right from the start.

If you are ready to get started with the creation of your own table, you will need to bring up the command of CREATE TABLE. You can then bring up the table, but make sure that you organize it nicely so that it will be easy to read through and will still work the way that you want.

However, before you go through and create a new table, you need to ask yourself a few questions about it. This will ensure that you are able to actually design the table in a manner that fits your needs, rather than just creating any old table and then having to spend a lot of time making fixes and more along the way. Some of the questions you should ask before making your own table includes:

- What is the best name for the table?

- What data do I plan to work on within the table?
  what column will I use in order to form the main key

- Which names should be assigned to the columns?

- What data type can I assign to these columns

- Which columns should I allow to be empty

- What length should I place as the maximum for every column?

Once you have taken some time to look over the questions above and answer all of them, you will just need to type in CREATE TABLE and then fill out the rest of the table. Also, you should make sure to remember that the last character in your statement needs to be a semicolon.

Almost all of the types of SQL that you can use will have certain characters that you are able to use in order to terminate or submit statements to the server. With the MySQL or Oracle programs, you will be able to do the semicolon in order to get these actions to happen while working with Transact-SQL is going to use the "GO" command to get this step done. We are going to stick with using the semicolons in this book for doing these things to keep them all in order.

Understanding the Storage Clause

At some time, you will find that there will be a need to work with the storage clause. This storage clause is going to be the one that will help us out a lot here because we can use it to assign the size that you would like to use with your table. This means that you will need to bring up and use the storage clause, even when we are still working on our new table and even during the creation process. You get to be in charge of this table, choosing whether it needs to get smaller or shrink down based on how you would like to use the table and what you are hoping the table inside your database will look like when it is done.

The Rules for Naming

While we are here, we need to take a look at some of the rules that need to come into play when it is time to name our able, as well as some of the other parts of the database. No matter which language of programming you are working with, whether it is SQL or another option out there, you have to learn the naming rules ahead of time so that you can write them out in a manner that the compiler will understand and can read.

When you are naming the various objects that are meant to show up in the database, especially with the tables and the columns, you will want to go with a name that is reflective of the data that you would like to put into that specific part of the code. For example, if you have started with a new table and you called it EMPLOYEES_TBL, you would expect that when you take a look at this there will be some sort of information about the employees inside. Make sure that you are going through and using the same idea when you would like to name the columns of the database.

How to Alter the Elements of the Table

As you go through and work on your table, you may notice that there are times when changes and modifications are going to be necessary for the different elements that are already present and written out in the table. the attributes of the columns are going to be the laws and the behaviors of any data that is found in that column.

However, you do get the chance to go through and change up the attributes that you want, and the process is actually pretty easy to work with. You can work with the SQL function of ALTER TABLE. To understand a few of the attributes and what each of them is supposed to be used for, here is a list of the attributes that we are referring to:

1. The type of data that you had already assigned to that column.
2. The scale, length, and even the precision of that column.
3. Whether the user is able to go through and enter the NULL value into each of these columns.

When you would like to make some adjustments that include adding in some more columns to the existing table that you have, you will need to go through and follow a few rules. One of these rules is that you should not add in a NOT NULL column if you notice that the table already holds onto some data. The reason for this is that the NOT NULL shouldn't be used in a manner that indicates that the column could hold some value for the rows in the data in the table.

If you get to this point and you try to add in a NOT NULL column at this point, you are basically going against some of the constraints that are already there. This ends up leading us to have some issues when you want to add in some of the specific values that you need at this point.

Following all of the rules that are needed in SQL and in some of the other programming languages to get some of your work done can be confusing on occasion. But you will find that these are going to ensure that you can pull up the right parts of the code at the right time. Some of the other important SQL rules that you need to remember when it is time to make modifications in the fields and columns inside of the SQL table will include:

- You can always increase the length of your column.

- You can decrease the length of the column only if the highest value of the column is lower or equal to the length that you desire.
- You can always make an increase in the number of digits that are allowed for the numeric data types.
- You are able to decrease the number of digits for these numeric data types only if the value of the largest amount of digits in the column will be lower or equal to the number of digits that you would like to add.
- You can decrease or increase the number of decimal places when you are using the numeric data types.
- You can make changes to any of the data types that are present for your column.

When you use these rules to make some small changes to the table, always be careful and pay attention to what you are working on at the time. If you do it in a hurry and do not pay attention, it is going to be easy to lose some of the information because of this. And unfortunately, the information can be really hard to get back, especially if it is something important like the address or a name of a client. So, this is why we need to pay some special attention at any time that we want to make changes that are necessary for our tables and databases.

Taking an Old Table and Using It to Create a New Table

Another step or tool that you may find as a useful thing when working in SQL is to learn how to take one of the tables that you already have, and then use this information to create a new table. There are actually two good commands that you are able to use to make this happen, including SELECT and CREATE TABLE so we are going to explore how those work now.

After you have been able to go through and execute the two commands above, you can then see that the new table that you were able to create is going to hold onto the same information, and will come with the same scope and definition, as the original database. This is a customizable feature that is important for you to work with so you can even choose what will come over from the old database to the new one. Sometimes you will want to bring over all of the information that you have, and sometimes you will just want to use it a little bit in the program and not all of that information.

The syntax that you are going to use in order to create this new table from the table that is already in the database includes:

CREATE TABLE NEW_TABLE_NAME AS
SELECT ["|COLUMN1, COLUMN2]

FROM TABLE_NAME

[WHERE];

As you can see, the new syntax that you are working on is going to use the SELECT keyword. This is the keyword that you should use any time that you would like to work on a query inside of the database. This SELECT keyword is also going to make it easier to work on the new table, and creating a new one, with the search results.

How to Drop Tables

Dropping a table is going to be one of the other processes that you are able to work within SQL. If you decide to use the RESTRICT statement, and then reference a table by working with view or constraint, then the DROP command is going to provide you with a message that there is some kind of error going on in the system. But you can use the CASCADE command in order to get the DROP command to work, and when this is used, then all of the views and the constraints can be dropped at this time. The syntax that we are able to use to help us to drop our new table will be below:

DROP TABLE TABLE_NAME [RESTRICT | CASCADE]

Whenever you are dropping a new database table, you will need to take the time to specify the name of the owner of the table that you want to work on. This is going to be important because if you end up dropping the wrong table, you will lose some of the data that is inside the table. If you have the access of the database accounts for more than just your account, make sure that you have already logged into the right account, and not just on yours if the database is in a different place, so that you aren't making changes in the wrong account.

The Integrity Constraints

Some of the times when you are working with SQL, it is possible that we will need to bring up the integrity constraints to help ensure that the data that we are putting into our tables and our database will not only be accurate but also consistent as well. In many situations, the user who is on the database is going to have to work on this integrity through a process that is known as referential integrity. We will quickly find that there are a few different tools that we are able to use with this kind of concept to make it easier to maintain the integrity of the database, and a few of them that you may find as the most useful here will include:

The Primary Key

The first integrity constraint that we need to take a look at is the primary key. These are going to be the ones that we use in order to make some of our rows unique. You can form one of these keys if you only are working with one column, but for the most part, it doesn't come out until you have more than one to work with.

For example, you will be able to make an assigned reference number, or the name of your product, one of the primary keys inside of a table that you created. The goal that we are trying to reach with the primary key is to provide each of the records with a unique detail, which is going to make them easier to find later on. You will be able to keep things simple when you decide to create the primary key that you need when you first create the table, rather than doing it later on and trying to fix things later on.

Unique Column Restraints

The second option that we need to look at here is going to be similar to what we just talked about with the primary keys since the columns have to hold onto a unique value with each row. While we need to make sure that we are placing this primary key inside of each of the columns, it is possible to use the unique column constraints to help us to place this constraint that we just made up into two different columns if that is needed.

The Foreign Key

We can also spend some time working with the foreign key if we would like, especially when we end up in a situation where we need to work with both the parent table and the child table. These foreign keys are going to be the columns that are found on the child table, but these specifically point back to their own primary key, which we should find on the parent table that we worked in the first place.

This type of key is going to become one of our main tools when it is time to check out whether the integrity standards that you set were actually met in the database that we are working with. You will be able to use the column for the foreign key as a way to reference the key that is inside of the second kind of table when this is needed.

Drop Constraints

The next thing that we need to focus on is drop constraints. These are going to work in a slightly different manner compared to what we are going to find with some of the other options, but you will find that they are going to be useful when it is time to change up a few of the other constraints that are inside of your database or table already.

For example, you may work on a database where you would need to drop the primary key that is in one table. And to make this happen, we would have to pull out our drop constraints feature. Just remember that you will need to work with the DROP CONSTRAINT command and then it will tell the compiler to drop the right constraint that you choose whether you are looking to drop the unique column restraints, the foreign key, or the primary key.

Any time that you decide to drop one of the constraints, we have to remember that we are deleting it permanently, rather than just setting it to the side until later. So, before we go through and try to do this, we have to make sure that the constraint that we are trying to get rid of is one that you actually want to discard and no longer use. There are some situations where deleting that constraint is a good option, but there is also the option to just disable the constraint, rather than deleting it, so you need to decide which one is going to be the best for your needs.

If you plan to use one of the constraints later, then disabling them is going to be the best option. If you plan to not use them any longer in this database, then it is best to cut them out or drop them. It often depends on what you plan to do within the code. Disabling them is sometimes better because you are able to turn them off in areas where you do not need them, but then you are able to go back through and reactivate them when you would like.

 There are going to be a lot of objects that you are able to place into the database to keep it organized and to ensure that you are provided a seamless experience for your user. You will be able to use some of the commands that are in this chapter to help to make the tables work just how you would like them and to make sure that all the information that you would need inside the database for easy access and use.

Chapter 5: Search Queries in SQL

Now that we have had some time to work with some of the different parts that come with doing a database in SQL, it is time to go through and do a search over that database to find the information that you really need. This is going to be one of the best steps to find the information that you need, but originally, without the right commands, you will find that the database is not really going to be set up in order to make searches as easy as we would like. And you need to be able to set up your database in a way so that it is able to provide fast and accurate results back to the customer when they do a search.

A good way for us to think about this is like when we have a customer go to our website, and they want to do a search for a specific product that they want. Do you want to make sure that you have a database that is set up slow and brings up a bunch of results that really have nothing to do with what the customers want? Or would you rather have a database that is fast and efficient, and provides the perfect products for the customer to pick from? This is why we are going to spend some time in this guidebook taking a look at how to get some of these queries in the database to provide you with some of the results that you want with your own database to the customers.

Working on the Queries

When you are ready to do your own query or do a search, you are basically starting a process where you send out an inquiry to the database that is already set up. You can get this done with the help of the SELECT command and you have to add this in front of all the queries that you are going to give to the database.

So, if you are on a table that is going to hold onto all of the products of the company inside of that database, you would then be able to use the SELECT command to find the product that is on this table. Perhaps you want the one that is considered the best selling or the one that meets another type of criteria that the customer is looking for. the request is going to be good for all of the products that are usable on the database. And the relational databases that you want to work with will be able to make this work in no time.

Working with the SELECT Command

Remember that when we would like to complete one of these queries in our database, the SELECT command is going to be the one that we need to use in order to see this happen. The SELECT command is going to be the one that is in charge of starting, and then executing, all of the queries that you are sending out. in many situations, we need to not just type in the SELECT command though. We need to tell the compiler what we want it to SELECT so it knows what answers to work with. You could do something like adding in the name of the product that you want, and maybe a few descriptive features that are going to come with it as well to get the results that you want from that SELECT command.

Whenever you decide to work with the SELECT command that is inside of this language, there are four main keywords that we need to focus on. These are going to be known in SQL as the four clauses, and they need to be present in order to finish off your command and bring back the item that you want. These four keywords in SQL are going to include:

- SELECT—this command will be combined with the FROM command in order to obtain the necessary data in a format that is readable and organized. You will use this to help determine the data that is going to show up. The SELECT clause is going to introduce the columns that you would like to see out of the search results and then you can use the FROM in order to find the exact point that you need.

- FROM—the SELECT and the FROM commands often go together. It is mandatory because it takes your search from everything in the database, down to just the things that you would like. You will need to have at least one FROM clause for this to work. A good syntax that would use both the SELECT and the FROM properly includes:

  ○ SELEC [* | ALL | DISTINCT COLUMN1, COLUMN2]

- o FROM TABLE1 [, TABLE2];

- WHERE—this is what you will use when there are multiple conditions within the clause. For example, it is the element in the query that will display the selective data after the user puts in the information that they want to find. If you are using this feature, the right conditions to have along with it are the AND and OR operators. The syntax that you should use for the WHERE command includes:

  - o SELEC [* | ALL | DISTINCT COLUMN1, COLUMN2]

  - o FROM TABLE1 [, TABLE2];

  - o WHERE [CONDITION1 | EXPRESSION 1]

  - o [AND CONDITION2 | EXPRESSION 2]

- ORDER BY—you are able to use this clause in order to arrange the output of your query. The server will be able to decide the order and the format that the different information comes up for the user after they do their basic query. The default for this query is going to be organizing the output going from A to Z, but you can make changes that you would like. The syntax that you can use for this will be the same as the one above, but add in the following line at the end:

- ○ ORDER BY COLUMN 1 | INTEGER [ASC/DESC]

Remember that we need to use all of these, and see them all in place if we want to make sure that the SELECT command is being used in the proper manner and that it actually pulls up the right information that we are searching for with any query you do in your database.

Handling the Case Sensitivity

While case sensitivity is going to be very important when we are working with some of the other coding languages that are out there, you will find that it is not going to be as important when we are working with the SQL language. You are able to focus on the upper case and lower-case words as you would like, and often you are able to use either type of letter in order to set up the names that you would like inside of the columns. It is even possible for us to enter in the statements and the clauses in either of these two cases, without having to worry about whether or not they will work in this language.

Now with this said, there may be a few times when we do need to worry about this kind of sensitivity in this language more than the other times. One of the main times that we need to pay attention and focus on this is with the data objects. Most of the data that we want to store in our database should be done with the help of uppercase letters. This is going to make it easier to maintain some consistency in what you are doing in the database.

For example, you may end up with some issues if one of the users is typing in JOHN for their name, and the other one types in John and then the third types in john. If you set up some rules about the case sensitivity here, you will find that it is actually easier to keep the database organized and working well, and it will be a lot easier for the user to find and get the relevant information that they need each time.

In many cases, working with the upper-case letters is going to be one of the most efficient methods to make this happen because it is easier to work with, and the user will be used to this when they have worked with some of the other databases in the past. If you choose to not focus on the upper-case option, you should find some other method of working with case sensitivity in a consistent manner. This will make it easier for your users to have a chance of figuring out what they are doing in the database, and they can figure out the system faster than ever.

These transactions, as well as some of the queries that come with them, are going to be really important when we are trying to make sure that our database, and the system as a whole, is going to perform the way that we want. You may feel that this is not that big of a deal and that the user and yourself will be able to find all of the information in a quick manner without setting up this good query, but doing it in this manner is just going to leave everyone feeling really confused and frustrated in the process.

It is much better for you and the others who are using this system if you go through and use SQL to set up a good search query. This makes it so that your customers are able to find the product they need, and it could be as simple as using a search bar to type in keywords or the specific product that they want. And you get the assurance that the customer is going to be happy with the products that they are getting, and with the experience that they have with your particular database.

Another integral part of the database that you are working with for your business is the transactions. And if the transactions on the database are not working properly, it can really harm the profits of your business. There are many times when the user, or even you, will need to take a look at some of the information. You can, if the database is set up well, go through the table and find out whether some of the information is needed to change, or if you are able to look up some of the information that you need.

There are also going to be some situations when the user is going to be willing to look up a bit of information when they just perform a search. And when the search is done, and the database is set up in the proper manner, they will be able to get all of the information that they need. The user is going to prefer it if you are able to set up the database to make it easier to find the exact match that you want right away. This is much preferable to continuing to search and having to put in a bunch of keywords throughout and trying again and again to find the keywords that we need.

Either way that we decide to work with the database, it is so important that we make sure that the commands end up in the right place, and that we can find the table set up in the proper manner so that both you, and anyone else who works with the database, will be able to find what they would like faster. This chapter is going to provide us with some of the commands that we need, and all of the other information that is important when it is time to help us handle the transactions and get things done within the database that we are working with.

Chapter 6: The Concept of Relational Databases

The next topic that we need to explore here is the idea of a relational database. A relational database is going to be one of the types of databases that are able to store and provide us with access to any of the data points that are related to one another. Relational databases are based on the relational model and an intuitive straightforward way of representing data in tables. In this kind of database, each row in the table is going to be a record with a unique ID that is called the key. The columns of the table will hold onto the attributes of the data, and each record usually has a value that is going to be handed to each attribute, making it easy to establish the relationship among data points.

How Relational Databases are Structured

The relational model means that we are going to work with structures of logical data, the data tables, views, and the indexes, and we will separate them out from some of the physical structures of storage that we are using. What this kind of storage is going to mean is that the administrators of the database will be able to manage the physical storage in the manner that they would like, without having to really affect access to that data at all. They can add items and change items, and the customer will still be able to get into the system and use it. For example, renaming a file of the database is not going to do anything o rename the tables that are stored inside.

The distinction that we are going to find between the physical and the logical is also going to apply to the operations of the database which are clearly defined actions that are going to enable applications to manipulate the data and structures of the database. Logical operations will allow our application to specify the content that it needs, and the physical operations will determine how that data needs to be accessed and then carries out the task.

During this process, while ensuring that the data is always accurate and accessible, the relational databases are going to follow certain rules of integrity. For example, an integrity rule can specify that duplicate rows should not happen in the table. This will help make sure that information that is erroneous is not going to show up in our database.

The Relational Model

In some of the earlier years of the database, every application stored data in its own unique structure. When developers wanted to be able to build the application to use that data, they had to know about the structure of a particular type of data before they were even able to find the kind of data that is needed. These data structures were not all that efficient, they were really hard for the programmer to maintain, and hard to optimize when it was time to deliver good application performance. This kind of model was designed to solve the problem that came up when we had many arbitrary data structures.

The relational model was able to provide us with a standard way to represent and even to query some of the data that can be used in any kind of application that we would like. From the beginning, many developers recognized that the biggest strength of this model was the use of the tables. These tables were going to be intuitial, flexible, and efficient and could help to store and access all of the structured information that we need.

Over time, there was another big strength that came out when we were looking at the relational model. This happened when we say more use of the SQL or structured query language, to write and query in this database. For many years, this language has been used to help out with a database query. Based on the idea of relational algebra, SQL is going to provide us with an internally consistent mathematical language that is going to help us to improve the performance that we will see with all database queries. In comparison, most of the other approaches are not going to be as efficient.

The Benefits of These Relational Databases

The simple yet powerful relational model is going to be used by organizations of all types and sizes for a lot of their informational needs. Relational databases are going to be used to help out track inventories, process some of the transactions of eCommerce, manage a lot of information about the customer, and so much more. A relational database can be considered for any information need where the company is going to have the data points relate to one another and must be managed in a consistent, rules-based, and secure manner.

There are a lot of options that we are able to see when it is time to work with these kinds of databases. Some of the biggest benefits that we are going to see with using these will include:

Data Consistency

The relational model that we are talking about here is going to be the best when we want to maintain the consistency of the data through different applications and copies of the database, also known as instances. For example, when a customer goes through and deposits money into an ATM, and then they want to take a look at that balance on a phone, the customer is going to expect that the deposit is there on heir account. The relational databases excel at this kind of data consistency, ensuring that multiple instances of a database have the same data all of the time.

It is sometimes difficult for the other types of database to really stick with this level of consistency, especially in a timely manner, when we are looking at large amounts of data. Some of the more recent databases that have come out, including NoSQL, can support only what is known as eventual consistency.

Under this particular principle, when the database is scaled, or even when there is more than one user getting to the same data at the same time, we will find that the data has to take some time to play catch up. Eventual consistency is going to be acceptable for some users, such as to help us maintain some of the listings that we have in a product catalog. But when it comes to some of the critical operations of the business, such as working with the transactions in a shopping cart, the relational database is going to be the best.

Stored Procedures

You will find that data access is going to involve us going through a lot of repetitive actions. For example, just to complete a simple query to get information from our data table could be repeated hundreds or thousands of times just to get the results that we want. These data access functions will need us to work with some code to help access the database that we are working with.

The developers of an application do not want to go through and write out some new code for these functions each time that they start a new application. Luckily these databases are going to come out and will be able to store some of these procedures. Then you can use them as blocks of code that we can access with a simple call of the application.

For example, a single stored procedure is able to provide us with a consistent tagging record for the users in more than one application at a time. Stored procedures are also going to help developers to ensure that certain functions of data in that specific application are going to be implemented in the manner that you want.

Database locking and concurrency

There are times when some conflicts can arise in a database when there are many users or applications that are working to change up the same data in that database, especially when these are happening at the same time. locking and concurrency techniques are going to help reduce the potential for conflicts while maintaining how much integrity is going to be found in the data.

Locking is going to prevent other applications and users from accessing the data while it is being updated. In some of the databases, you will find that locking is going to apply to the entire table, which is going to create a negative impact on the application performance. Other databases that you can choose to work with, including the Oracle relational databases, are going to apply these locks at the record level, which is going to leave some of the other records that are inside of this table available. Overall, this is going to make sure that we get the application to performance to improve.

And then we can look at concurrency. This is the part that is going to manage the activity when there are more users or applications that invoke queries at the same time, on the same database. These capabilities are going to provide us the right access to the users and the applications based on what kinds of policies that we would have with data control.

What Should I Look for When Picking a Relational Database?

The software that we are going to use to store, manage, query, and then retrieve the data that is stored in a relational database is going to be known as the RDBMS, or the relational database management system. This is going to provide us with an interface between users and applications and the database, as well as some of the administrative functions to help us manage how we store our data, access the data, and how that data performs.

There are going to be a few different factors can help to guide our decisions when it is time to choose which of the many available databases types that we want to go with. The RDBMS that you will want to go with will depend on your business needs and how we will use it. Some of the questions that we need to ask when it is time to make a decision about all of this includes:

1. What are the requirements for data accuracy? Will the storage and accuracy of our data depend on the business logic? Does the data we are using have some really strong requirements when it comes to accuracy levels? These could include things like financial information or government reports.

2. Do we need scalability? We also have to take a look at the scale of the data that we want to manage, and what the anticipated growth is all about. The model of the database needs to support some of the mirrored copies of the database to help with scalability. And if it does, can it maintain data consistency across all of these instances.

3. How important is the idea of concurrency for us? Will there be a need for multiple applications and users to get the data at the same time? Will the software that we are using for this database support this concurrency while protecting the data?

4. What are some of our performance and reliability needs? DO you need to work with a product that is a really reliable and high performance? What are some of the requirements that we have when it comes to query response performance? What do we see when it comes to the commitments of the vendor for some of the service level agreements or some of the downtime that happens that is not planned.

Working with a relational database is one of the best things that you are able to do when it comes to working with some of the databases that you need to handle in your business. There are certainly other types of databases that are out there, but none are going to provide you with the power, the efficiency, the consistency, and more that you need, in order to really make sure that the database is going to work when you want it to.

Chapter 7: How to Categorize Our Information with the Database Operators

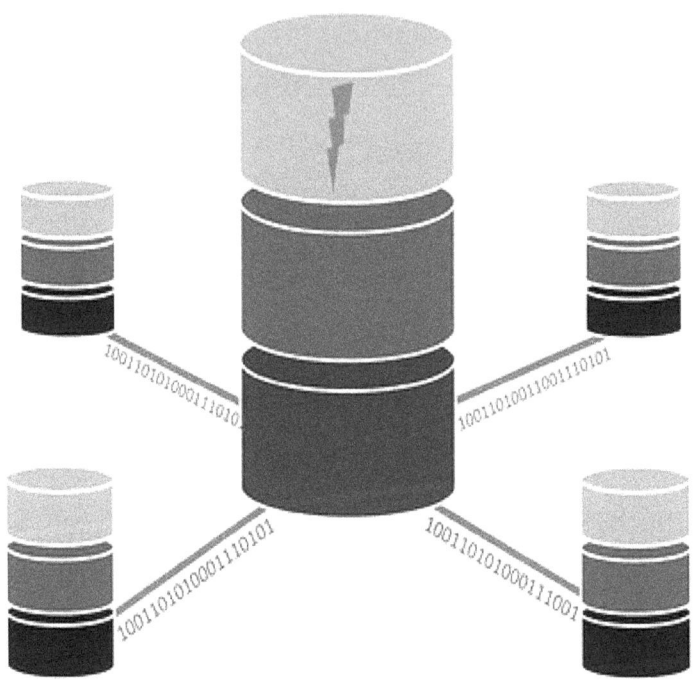

There are going to be some times when you work with a database and you find that it is helpful to categorize the information that is inside of that database. This can make it a lot easier for you to find the information later on and will ensure that our database is organized rather than having all of the parts all over the place. This is why we are going to spend some time in this chapter looking at how we can categorize with the help of the database operators so that everything stays in its place.

Through this chapter, when we bring up the topic of the operators that are inside of the database, we are going to talk about the characters and the words that we have reserved, and any that can be used along with the WHERE clause of the statements we write. Operators are helpful because we are able to use them to perform operations in the statements, such as comparisons and any of the equations that we need in math, but they can also come in to make it easier to set up some of the parameters that we want to see around our statements. And we need to always remember that they are there to help us connect together two or more parameters that we have in the same statement if this is something that our code needs.

During this process, we are going to need to remember that there are a few options of operators that you are able to use in these statements. The four most common options that we are able to work with include:

1. Operators that are used to help negate conditions.
2. Logical operators

3. Comparison operators
4. Arithmetic operators.

We will quickly see that each of these will be important inside of the statement that we are trying to work with, and will help to ensure that your parameters are going to work in the manner that we want. You will need to choose the right one to use at the right time so that we get the results that we need. And doing these steps and taking these precautions will ensure that we are not going to get an error message to show up.

The Logical Operators

The first operator type that we are going to spend some time focusing on in this guidebook will be the logical operators. These are going to be the kinds of operators that we are able to use with the keywords of our statements, and they are going to be easier to form with comparisons inside of the statements. Some of the different logical operators that we are able to add into our statements will include:

- In—this operator will allow you to compare the value of specified literal values that are set. You will get a true if one or more of the specified values is equal to the value that you test.

- Like—the like operator is going to make it so that you can compare a value against others that are similar. You will usually combine it with the "_" or the "%" sign to get more done. The underscore is used to represent a number or a character ad the % is used for several characters, zero, or one.

- Unique—with the unique operator, you will be able to take a look at one or more of your data rows and see if they are unique or not.

- Exists—you will need to use this operator to find the data rows that will meet the criteria that you put down. It basically allows you to put down some criteria and see if there are any rows that exist that meet with this.

- Between—you can use this operator in order to find values that will fall into a specific range. You will need to assign the maximum and the minimum values to make this work.

- Is null—the is null operator will allow you to compare the value of your choosing with a NULL one.

- Any and all—any and all values often go together. Any operator is going to compare a value against all of the values on a list. The list of values is to be set up with predetermined conditions. ALL, on the other hand, will compare the values that you select against the values that are in a different value set.

These are good operators to learn how to use because they will help us to make some good comparisons and to help us look at a few of the points of data that are already inside of our database that we are working with. You are able to work with a few of these logical operators and see how they can work with some of the different statements that you want to work with, and see what will be the best for you.

The Comparison Operators

The second operator that we are able to work with inside of the SQL language is going to be the comparison operators. These are going to be the ones that you would choose to use when you want to check on some of the single values that are found in the statement here. This category is going to be composed of a few mathematical signs, some that you are even familiar with so it is not going to be too hard for us to figure out. Some of the best comparison operators that we are able to work within this database will include:

- Non-equality—if you are testing the non-equality operator, you will use the "<>" signs. The operation is going to give you the result of TRUE if the data does not equal and FALSE if the data does equal. You can also use the "!=" to check for this as well.

- Equality—you will be able to use this operator in order to test out some single values in your statement. You will simply need to use the "=" sign to check for this. You are only going to get a response if the data that you chose has identical values. If the values aren't equal, you will get a false and if they are equal, you will get a true.

- Greater-than values and Less-than values—these two are going to rely on the "<" and ">" signs to help you out. They will work as stand-alone operators if you would like but often, they are more effective when you combine them together with some of the other operators.

These are going to help us to see some of the single values that are found in any of the statements of our database, and sometimes they are able to bring out some unique things like the less than and great than options, resulting in a few true and false statements that add in some power to the code we are writing and can make our program stronger than ever before.

Arithmetic Operators

The third type of operator that we need to focus on is going to be the arithmetic operator. These are going to be the most useful when we are trying to add in some of the different mathematical operations that are useful in the SQL language. There are going to be four main arithmetic operators that we are able to use inside of these equations, and we are able to combine a few of them together in the same statement if that is what is needed for our code. The four main types of operators that we are able to focus on here will include:

- Addition—you will just need to use the "+" sign to get started on using addition. For this example, we are going to add up the values for the overhead column and the materials column. The statement that works for this is:

  - SELECT MATERIALS + OVERHEAD FROM PRODUCTION_COST_TBL.

- Subtraction—you can also do some basic subtraction when it comes to your SQL statements. You will simply need to use the "-" sign to do this.

- Multiplication—it is possible to do multiplication from your tables as well. You would need to use the "*" sign to do this.

- Division—this one will just need the "/" sign to get started.

With the arithmetic operators, you will be able to gain a lot of freedom in some of the codes that you are writing. You can combine a few of these operators together and even end up with your own equation inside of the statement. For example, you could have one statement with a bit of multiplication along with some division and addition if you would like. You can also have it so that you are just using a few multiplication signs in the same statement as well. Whatever is needed to bring the code together and make it work in the way that you want is available when it comes to these arithmetic operators.

One thing that we need to remember when we decide to add in more than one of these operators to our statement at a time is that we need to work with something known as the principles of precedence to make sure that we get it right. This means that the syntax is going to be able to take care of the arithmetic operators in a certain way to help us get the right answer.

When we are doing this kind of principle in SQL, the syntax is going to take care of everything that we need to multiply first, and then it will pay attention to everything that we need to divide, and then it will do those that should be added together, before finishing up with the things that should be subtracted from one another. And the syntax is going to do this in a manner that goes from left to right, along with going through the symbols in the order that we did above. This makes sure that we are going to get the right answers, and is similar to what we should remember from basic algebra classes in the past.

What Operators Are Important When Negating Conditions?

As we are working through this kind of code, there may be some situations where we will need to negate the operators that are in the database. This is going to be important because it will change up the viewpoint that this condition will have. It is possible to do this with the NOT command because it helps us to cancel out some of the original use of the operator. You may want to spend a bit of time trying out a few of these operators in order to negate the conditions and see what we are able to do with them. Some of the techniques that are the most useful with this one when we want to negate our conditions from the start will include:

- Not equal—you can use this when you want to find the results that are not equal to something. For example, if you did use the "<>" or the "!=" symbols you would get anything that was not equal to the value that you placed into the equation.

- Not between—you can also negate with the not between and the between operators. For example, if you are using a price, you could decide that you want to find the values that are not between 500 and 1000 or any value. This means that all the values that come up need to be either 499 and below or 1001 and above.

- Not in—if you will be able to use the not in command in order to negate the in operator. You will be able to ick some values that you don't want to have listed and then the not in command will return you anything that doesn't fit in that amount.

- Not like—this is the term that you will use to negate the operator like. When you are using this, you are only going to see the values that are different from the one that you placed into the equation.

- Is not null—this one will work to negate the is a null command. You will want to use this in order to check for the data that isn't null.

These operators are going to be useful because they will help us to set up the conditions that we need the most inside of the statements, and can also work well inside some of the searchers that we want to complete as well. This helps us to bring back all of the information that we need from the database with just one simple search in the process.

Working with the Conjunctive Operators

Another type of operator that we need to spend some of our time on here is the conjunctive operators. When you are doing some work with your statements, you may find that there will be some times when new criteria will be needed in order to make sure that the command is going to behave the way that we want.

For example, if you are sending out a database search and your results that might be a bit more confusing, you may find that adding in some different criteria to the mix to get the results you want is a much better idea. You can also use these when you would like to be able to combine together a few different types of criteria within the single statement, and then you would create a brand-new conjunctive operator that works for your needs.

Even though you are able to technically create one of the conjunctive operators that you want, there are going to be a few of these that are already predefined inside of the SQL language, and you are able to use them as you need. Some of these operators are going to include:

- OR—you will use this statement to combine the conditions of the WHERE clause. Before this statement can take action, the criteria need to be separated by the OR or it should be TRUE.

- AND—this operator is going to make it easier to include multiple criteria into the WHERE section of your statement. The statement will then only take action when the criteria have been segregated by the AND and they are all true.

As with some of the other operators that you will run across, you are able to combine these together inside of the same statement and you can even have more than one of the same conjunctive operators in the statement as well if you would like. You should take care to add in some parentheses when you are using these to help improve some of the readability in the statement.

These operators are all important and each of the categories is going to make a big difference in what we are able to do with some of our own statements. You are able to use the arithmetic operators to help with mathematical equations, work on how to compare different parts of the database, and so much more. You will not have to work longer with the SQL language in order to see all of the cool things that you are able to do with this language in no time at all.

Chapter 8: Keeping Your Database Secure

We have spent a lot of time in this guidebook taking a look at how to create these databases and all of the different things that we are able to do with these databases. We are going to be able to use a lot of different commands to help us out with this, and we will find that these databases are going to be able to hold onto a lot of information inside of them and the SQL language is going to help us to get the results that we want out of this database.

Now that we know all of this information, it is time for us to take a look at how we are able to beef up some of the security of our database. If you are holding onto a lot of the customer data or transactional data that helps your business to grow and do well, you really need to make sure that this data is as safe as possible, and that no one who doesn't have access is going to be able to get ahold of that information.

We have heard a lot of stories where companies did not do a good job of keeping these databases secure. This ended up in some huge data breaches for the company and made it hard for the user to keep their own personal information safe. This has been enough to make it hard to keep these companies going and many times it can be enough to make them go out of business because they lost the trust they needed from their customers.

Of course, we do not want something like this to happen to our own businesses, so we need to make sure that all of the information that we place on our databases are going to be as safe as possible. Many times when we are going to hear about security and privacy advice for things online, we are going to spend time talking about the basics like having a password that is strong, backing up the data, using the right security applications, keeping the system up to date, and avoiding some of the default settings.

For the most part, these are going to be seen as the most essential and basic precautions that any manager of one of these systems has to pay attention to and try to use as well as possible. However, depending on what kind of system you would like to protect along the way, there are going to be a few other issues that we need to take into account, especially when it is time to handle the databases that we are working with.

Considering there is an alarming amount of frequency that comes with theft and leaks in information and databases, there are a few other techniques and tips that we are able to work with to keep the information on our databases as safe and possible. Some of the best ways that we are able to keep our information as safe and secure as possible will include:

Have Some Control Over Who Accesses the Database

The number one thing that you are able to do when it is time to work with the protection and the security of your database is making sure that you add in some control over who can access the database or not. When a lot of people are able to get access to the database, and they start to meddle in something, you will find that the result is never going to be a positive one. This allows for a lot of different issues to show up, and the more access you allow the harder it is for us to handle or notice when the wrong person is on the system.

The more that you are able to limit some of the privileges and the permissions that are on the system, the better it is for everyone. This is the same idea that is going to apply to the databases that are out there. When it comes to your database, you will find that the more that you are able to limit some of the privileges and permissions of those who can get on the database, the better.

The best solution that we are going to see here is that we need to have some rigorous access control. This is important because it is one of the first steps that we are able to use in keeping attackers away from the information. In addition to some of the permissions that are basic for your system, we need to continue a few other things including:

1. Limiting the amount of access, or who can access, the sensitive data for both the procedures of the database and the users. This means that your company should only authorize certain users and procedures to make some queries relating to some of the sensitive information that we are working with.

2. Limiting the use of the key procedures and only allowing specific users to be able to do this.
3. Whenever it is possible, you should make sure that there is an avoidance of simultaneous use and access that happens outside of some of the normal office hours that are going on.

Another good idea that we are going to see here is that you should take a look at all of the procedures and services that are not being used that often, or at least at the time, and disable them as much as possible. This is a good option to work with in order to make sure that these are not going to be attacked and used to access other parts of the database as well.

In addition, when it is possible, you need to put your database in some location that is on a server that is not accessible directly from the internet. This makes it a lot harder for a hacker or someone else to gain the access that they want from that system and will make it harder for any of that information from being exposed to some of the remote attackers who want to use that information.

Identify the Data That Is Sensitive and Critical

One of the first steps that we are able to take when it comes to working on our database and making sure that it is as secure as possible is to work on identifying the data that is the most sensitive and the most critical. This should be done even before considering some of the protection techniques and tools. This is going to help us to see what information, above all of the other information that is found in the database, is going to be the most important and should be protected the most.

To help us get this done, it is also very important for us to understand some of the logic and some of the architecture that comes with the database. This is helpful because it is going to tell us more about where and how the data that is the most critical and the most sensitive should be stored.

While there may be a lot of different parts that come with the database that you work with, it is important to note that not all of the data that we are holding onto and storing will be that critical, and not all of it is going to need some protection. This means that it is not going to make a lot of sense for us to spend our time, our money, or our resources on this type of information.

We need to go through and figure out which information is actually the most important for what we want to get done with some of our coding. We need to be able to focus on the data that could put us or our customers at risk along the way. If the hacker gets the name of the customer and their age, they probably won't get too far. But if they get their name, social security number and credit card information, it is going to be a bad thing. Learning what information is important and being careful about what kind we are supposed to keep safe is important.

It is also important during this step to make sure that we keep a good inventory of the databases of the company being sure that we actually take all of the departments that we are working with into account. The only way to administer and make sure that we do not lose out on important information along the way is to effectively know all about the company's instances and all of the databases that are there. For many of the bigger companies, there are going to be quite a few databases out there, and keeping a good record of them, and knowing what is on them, can really help out here.

What's more, we also need to make sure that we get an inventory because it is going to be really useful when it is time to do a backup of the information that we have. This is going to make sure that in this process, we are not going to end up leaving some critical data out of what we are doing.

Make sure to take some time to look through the data that you have and figure out what is most important. Think about what would happen if the hacker was able to get ahold of a specific type of data, and whether it is time for us to hide it or not. When you focus more on how you are able to protect some of the data that is the most important, you can see the best way to use up your resources the way that they should, without letting some of the sensitive information get out there.

Encrypt Information

When we are working with a database, or any information that we want to keep secure, encryption is going to be one of your best friends. Once the data that is sensitive and confidential has been identified, it is going to be a good practice to work with some of the robust algorithms that are present in order to help encrypt that data as much as possible.

When an attacker tries to exploit some of the vulnerabilities that are found in the server, in the hopes of getting onto that system or server, the first thing that they will work on to steal is the databases. This is because the hacker will find that the database is a very valuable treasure. These databases, especially with some of the bigger companies out there, is going to contain many gigabytes of valuable information that we can use.

If the hacker is able to get onto the system that you are working with, you will find that it is going to be detrimental to your business and what you are doing. It is always best for you to go through and protect the database that you have by making it illegible to anyone who is trying to access it without having the right kinds of authorization ahead of time to be on there.

There are a lot of different methods that you are able to use when it is time to encrypt the data that is in the database. The amount of data that you are working with inside of that database, some of the regulations and rules that are in your industry when it comes to this data, and even some of the data that you are working with can help you to determine which rules of encryption you want to work with. You just need to make sure that the method of encryption that you are trying to work with is going to work, that it is secure, and that it is really going to make sure that those who should not be on the system or the database are not able to get onto it at all.

Anonymize the Non-Productive Databases

The next thing that we are going to take a look at when it is time to make sure that your database is safe and secure is to anonymize some of the databases that are not considered productive. Many companies are going to make sure that they invest their resources and time in protecting some of their productive databases, but when they are trying to develop a project or they want to create a test environment, they won't put in as much effort to take care of this. Instead, they are just going to copy the original database and then start to use it in an environment that is not as controlled as some of the others. This ends up with them exposing all of that sensitive information that is found in that database, without you even realizing what is going on.

That is why it is always a much better option for you to either mask or anonymize the database. This is going to be a process where a similar version is going to be created. You will be able to maintain the same structure as what you did originally, but you are able to modify some of the sensitive data so that it is going to stay as protected as possible. With this kind of technique, the values are going to be changed while still maintaining some of the formats that you would like.

The data that you are working with can be changed in a variety of manners. You can go through and mix it together. You can encrypt the data. And you can even mix up the characters that are found and substitute some of the words out to hide the meaning that is behind them.

The specific method that you decide to work with and the formats and rules that we need to respect each one is going to be up to what the administrator wants. But no matter what method you decide to use, you need to ensure that the process is one that is not reversible. And you need to go with one that, no matter what kind of reverse engineering is done on it, it will not allow someone to get onto that original data again without having the master copy of the database.

This is going to be a very commonly used, and even recommended, technique for any database that you are using as a part of an environment for testing and development. The reason for this is because it is going to allow you a way to preserve the logical structure of the data while still ensuring that the client information that is more sensitive is not going to ever be available outside of the production environment that you are working with.

Monitor the Activity on the Database

Another thing that we need to spend some time on in this guidebook and for ensuring that we are able to keep our database secure and the information of our customers as safe and secure as possible, is to monitor the activity that is happening on our database. Being aware of the auditing and recording actions, as well as the movement of the data means that you are going to have a clearer picture of what information has been handled when it is handled, how it is handled, and who is handling it.

Having a complete history of all of the transactions that happen in the database is also going to allow you to understand some of the access to the data, and can help with some of the modification patterns and can avid some of the more common issues and bigger problems that we are going to see including information leaks, helping you to control fraudulent changes, and detect suspicious activity in real-time.

Handling some of the security issues that can come up with the database that you are working with will be so important when it is time to make sure that your customers know they can trust you. If you are holding onto a lot of the credit card and payment information on your customers, you want to make sure that the wrong people are not able to take a look at that information and use it in their own manner.

That is why keeping the database you have as secure and safe as possible is going to be one of the best ways to ensure that you will be able to keep that information safe. And the fewer issues that you have when it comes to working with this kind of process, and the less likely it is that a hacker or someone else is going to get onto the database, the greater the trust you are able to build up with your customers, and the more likely it is that they will continue to work with you as well.

Chapter 9: Real World Applications of SQL

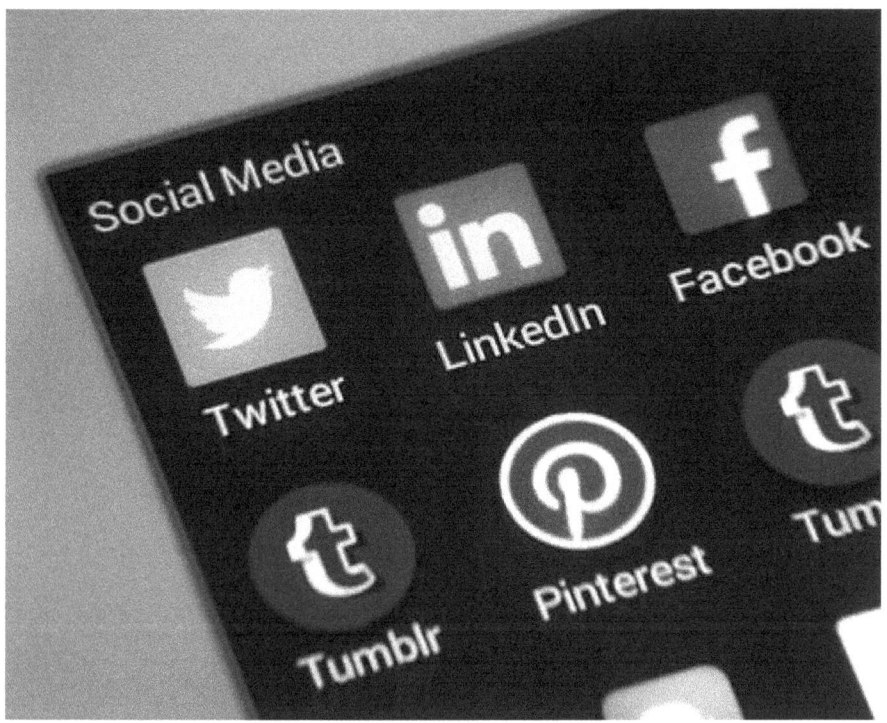

Before we close out on this subject, we need to bring out some of the uses that we are going to see with SQL today in our modern world. We will find that there are already a few real-world applications of this language that we are able to think about, just by taking a look at some of the information that we have been able to go through with this language overall. And you will find that there are so many others that we can focus on as well.

To start with, this language, SQL, is going to be used when we would like to take our relational database and retrieve the data or interface with the database as you need. It is a standard that was started in the 1970s, and because it is so effective and good at the job that it is supposed to help out with, you will find that it is still something that is around right now.

SQL is a popular method that we are able to use in order to get information out of our relational databases and the systems that they are on. These databases, as we talked about before, are going to be set up with a particular structure. In these relational databases, you will find that each record is going to have a series of keys that are going to be linked to one another in a manner that is very consistent and then they will place those values into a table that you are able to see in a visual manner on the grid.

This particular language is going to be written to comb the contents of the tables that are found in the conventional database. SQL is going to be used quite a bit when we talk about businesses, as well as other types of database administration. It is the default tool that we will see for operating with any of the conventional databases to help alter the data that is in the tables, retrieve the data that is there or manipulate the data that is on hand in another manner.

Some of the most simple commands that come with SQL will include those like INSERT, ORDER BY, and SELECT. All of these are going to usually be rendered in all capital letters to make it easier to stick with the syntax, and they are going to be there to help us to the administrator to route data in and out of that table of the database.

This is going on overall sorts of platforms, and it is going to be one of the main parts of helping us to deliver the results of data that we want in many of the modern cloud and hybrid systems of distribution. In the API economy that we are in right now, where so many pieces of our middleware are going to connect pieces join parts and an IT architecture, having SQL as the underlying database that is consistent and the best language to use is going to be central to helping us to port all of our data to the other places that need it at the time.

Because of the SQL coming with a really straightforward kind of syntax, and how easy this language is to use, administrators are able to focus less on the coding that they are doing, and can instead focus on how to construct the database and some of the logistical parts that come with getting the data into and out of the systems that they have. This makes it easier to work on some of the more important parts of the system, rather than hoping that you are able to get the language down and wasting weeks or months learning how to get it started.

Of course, even though there is a lot of popularity and use that is going to propel us with our databases, there are also a few alternatives to SQL that we are able to see. One of these is going to be known as NoSQL. This is a concept here that the data that is not tabled inside of the relational database my not really need to work with SQL as a query language.

So, the biggest users that you will see with SQL are going to be in a spectrum that can be called a smaller database system. Another way to help us to see how this is going to work is that the SQL language is not going to scale infinitely, even though there is a lot of uses for this language. With this kind of principle, the SQL is going to be used in a lot of situations for traditional DB systems when needed, and then there are going to be the need for other methods that are used for larger NoSQL database systems where checks on the data are not going to be enforced as much.

As we can imagine here, there are a lot of ways that we are able to use the SQL language to help us to make sure that we can use and manage the database that we are working with. The first method is that we are able to use SQL in order to help us to create a brand new database. Any time that you need to work with a new table, or a whole new database in the process, we will find that the SQL language can take it on and will get all of the information done for us in no time.

If you would like to make some modifications to some of the tables that you have in the database. Not only are you able to use this in order to add in some information and create the database that you want, but you can also use the SQL coding and some of the commands that you have in order to make some changes to the information. You can update some of the information, change it up, or even delete it if for some reason it no longer fits in with what you are doing.

And finally, we will find that it can be used to help us search through the database. If you want to find out more information on the customers you have in the database, you can use SQL. And if your customers would like to get on your website and find a specific product or something else they need, then the SQL language is going to be there to help out as well. If you want to make sure that your customers are able to find what they want and that they have the best experience possible online with your website, then you will want to work with the SQL language to make this happen.

There is so much that we are going to be able to do when we decide to work with the SQL language. But it is meant to help us really see some results with the databases that we are working with. There may be a few other options that you can use when it is time to handle one of the databases that you want to use, but when it comes to working with a coding language that is simple and can make working with your database, no matter how big or small, as easy as possible, then this is the best language to work with.

There are a lot of times when we are going to need to work with the SQL language. And when it comes to helping us to handle some of the work that we need to do within our databases and making it easier to manage some of the stuff that we need to do with our database, we will find that it is often one of the best languages to work with. No matter what kind of database we are dealing with at the time, we will find that these are going to be a great option to help us get started and will ensure that we are getting the exact right things out of them each time.

Conclusion

Thank you for making it through to the end of *SQL*, let's hope it was informative and able to provide you with all of the tools you need to achieve your goals whatever they may be.

The next step is to start working with some of the different parts that you are able to do with the help of the SQL language. Many medium and large companies are going to work with a database of some sort. Whether you use this to hold onto data that you will use later on to make some big decisions, you hold onto information about your customers, hold onto things about some of the products that you sell, or you use the database for some other reason, you will quickly find that there are so many uses for working on these databases.

Since many of these databases can be so large and have so many parts that come together in it, it is hard to imagine that we are going to be able to look through it manually to find everything that we need. This can sometimes make it difficult to do, and we will find that the SQL language is going to come in and help us. With some simple commands, simple enough that even those who have never worked with any kind of coding at all, will be able to pull up the different parts that they want out of the database.

This guidebook has taken some time to look at all of the neat things that you are able to do when it is time to work with the SQL language and see how this is going to work for some of our needs. There are many parts that come with this language and many new features that you can use to bring out exactly what you are looking for in the database that we are looking through. This guidebook will look at how we can explore the functions, objects, commands, and more that come with this language, and even the importance of working with some of the operators as well. All of these parts, along with some of the codes that we have spent some time on, will find that we are able to put all of the parts together in the right manner.

We will end out this guidebook with a look at some of the parts that we need to know in order to make sure that we are able to keep our database safe. So many databases are going to have sensitive information about the customer including their names, addresses, and even credit card information. And your business has to make sure that you are able to keep things as safe and secure as possible so that the customer feels safe shopping with you or keeping things in your database. We can then end with some of the real-world applications that we are going to see when it comes to working with this kind of coding language and making it work for our needs as well.

There are so many times when a company will need to work with a database in order to get the results that they want, to hold onto the right information to show the customers, and even to hold onto the information about the customer for future use. When we are able to combine together these databases with the SQL language, we will find that it is so much easier for you to handle and manage the database that you are working with. When you are ready to learn more about the SQL language and how it will help you with all of your database needs, make sure to check out this guidebook to help you get started.

Finally, if you found this book useful in any way, a review on Amazon is always appreciated!

Lightning Source UK Ltd.
Milton Keynes UK
UKHW021844260121
377731UK00003B/280